Mastering
Martial Arts

A Complete Guide to
JU JITSU

GIANCARLO BAGNULO

Enslow Publishing
101 W. 23rd Street
Suite 240
New York, NY 10011
USA
enslow.com

Published in 2018 by Enslow Publishing, LLC.
101 W. 23rd Street, Suite 240, New York, NY 10011

Library of Congress Cataloging-in-Publication Data
Names: Bagnulo, Giancarlo.
Title: A Complete Guide to Ju Jitsu / Giancarlo Bagnulo.
Description: New York, NY : Enslow Publishing, 2018. | Series: Mastering Martial Arts | Includes
bibliographical references and index. | Audience: Grades 7-12.
Identifiers: LCCN 2017001892 | ISBN 9780766085459 (library bound : alk. paper)
Subjects: LCSH: Jiu-jitsu--Juvenile literature.
Classification: LCC GV1114 .B33 2018 | DDC 796.815/2--dc23
LC record available at https://lccn.loc.gov/2017001892

Printed in the United States of America

To Our Readers: We have done our best to make sure all websites in this book were active and
appropriate when we went to press. However, the author and the publisher have no control over
and assume no liability for the material available on those websites or on any websites they may
link to. Any comments or suggestions can be sent by e-mail to customerservice@enslow.com.

Photo Credits: Cover © Olena Vasylkova (Nanka) | Dreamstime

All interior images © by DVE Publishing, worldwide, branch of Confidential Concepts, USA.

Contents

INTRODUCTION...5

HISTORY..7
  ‣ Historical Evolution of Ju Jitsu..7
  ‣ The Use of Ju Jitsu in the Past..8
  ‣ The Spread of Ju Jitsu..10
  ‣ The New Era of Ju Jitsu..11

DEFENSE TECHNIQUES AND LEGAL RESPONSIBILITY..........................13
  ‣ Criminal Liability During Training...13
  ‣ The Right to Defend Yourself...14

FIRST AID DURING TRAINING..16

JU JITSU CLASS..19

BASIC FUNDAMENTAL TECHNIQUES..24
  ‣ Kamae: Guards..24
  ‣ Ukemi Waza: Falling Techniques..27
  ‣ Atemi Waza: Striking Techniques...38
  ‣ Uke Waza: Blocking and Evasion Techniques................................50
  ‣ Kansetsu Waza: Levers and Joint Torsions...................................52
  ‣ Nage Waza: Throwing Techniques..56
  ‣ Shime Waza: Choking Techniques..61

Bare-Handed Defense Techniques
Against an Unarmed Aggressor...63

Bare-Handed Defense Techniques
Against an Armed Aggressor...95

Defense Techniques with Everyday Objects.............................111

Glossary...124

Further Reading...125

Index...126

Introduction

Ju jitsu (literally "flexibility technique" or more commonly known as "soft art") is a Japanese martial art that, due to the multiple blocking techniques it combines, is considered one of the most comprehensive disciplines for self-defense.

To fully understand the value of ju jitsu, a good starting point is to learn about the etymology of its name.

The ideogram representing *"ju"* signifies the principle of "flexibility," and is understood as the capacity to adapt oneself to different circumstances, taking advantage of the opponent's energy. To understand "ju," just imagine flexible branches bending under the weight of the snow and how they return to their natural state when the snow melts.

In contrast, the term *"jitsu"* means "science" or "art," and references the study and practice of combat techniques.

The breadth and complexity of this discipline should not dissuade the beginner, since the "ju" (the principle of flexibility) also makes reference to the possibility that any person approaching this martial art can learn it.

While learning ju jitsu, it is important to enlist the help of an expert, or Master. He or she will be able to guide you through the fundamental principles of the discipline in a way that is safe and geared toward your specific learning needs.

Obviously, one cannot study ju jitsu using only texts and videos— these resources are meant to act as supportive materials.

The objective of this book is not to highlight a specific school or particular method, but rather to introduce readers to the entire study of ju jitsu. Therefore one's knowledge of the combat method will become a resource to resolve situations that require defense from an aggressor.

Before exploring the most technical part of the book— the exercises themselves—it is important that you first reflect on the possible motivations that push people to approach or deepen their practice in this martial art. It is necessary for us to point out that while many people have good reasons for learning ju jitsu, some students are lured into the discipline by the unfortunate glorification of violence.

This attitude, entirely contrary to the spirit of ju jitsu, is clearly promoted by the violence inherent in modern combat sports, from which someone can extract misleading images about martial art disciplines as a whole.

Unfortunately, some schools, organizations, and private federations characterize violence, or the ability to exert violence, as a value of the discipline. These ideas have nothing to do with ju jitsu's sporting ethic; in fact, they threaten the physical integrity of the people trying to preserve it.

The promoters of these organizations take advantage of the insecurities that consume many people in certain moments of their lives; the instructors are presented as heroes with the capacity to teach everyone the secrets of self-defense and combat.

Cinema also contributes to the false conceptions about martial arts. This has been created by various forms of media, but especially by action movies, which have allowed martial arts to be interpreted by actors whose experience in combat sports has been highlighted solely for commercial purposes.

This book intends to provide an accurate depiction of the "soft art" ju jitsu as well as other combat sports.

History

Historical Evolution of Ju Jitsu

Nobody knows with absolute certainty when the codification of unarmed forms of defense, such as the *chikara* (power or influence), *kurabe* (the test of force), or *bu jutsu* (the art of combat), began in Japan. We do know, however, that ju jitsu's initial development was motivated by the increasing need for offensive and defensive military strength. Despite it's militaristic roots, ju jitsu has since been influenced and refined by religious, ethical, and philosophical factors.

The diversity of the technical concepts and standards was vital to the martial art from its origin, as was the need to establish coding to transmit the ideas over time.

After Japan's feudal era—which ranged from the Middle Ages to the Meiji period in the late nineteenth century—the samurai (warriors of the old range) were deprived of the right to carry the *katana* (saber or large *diasho*) and *wakizashi* (shorter saber or small diasho, also carried in the belt). During this period, the term ju jitsu generally referred to the forms of unarmed combat, occasionally practiced with weapons, that were taught in many *ryu* (schools of martial arts) spread throughout Japan. The founder (the *shodai* or *soke*) of martial arts disciplines also studied in these schools, and later the master, or *sensei*, of the ryu gave the best student (the *juko gashira*) the secret book or document (the *densho*), that contained secret information about the techniques of combat inherited from the old *bushi* (warriors).

The contents of this book could only be revealed to the followers of the school by the soke. The members of the clan guarded it with their lives, and it had different levels of disclosure within the ryu.

Only the most trusted disciples could access the more guarded *okuden* (secrets), while the rest of the students only had access to the *omote* (the most superficial part and the simplest concepts). Often, the juko gashira was the son of the shodai or sensei and received the title of *waka sensei* (young master).

There are many combat methods of the different ryu, and they allow followers to specialize in *toshunobu* techniques (unarmed defense against an unarmed aggressor), in the *bukinobu* (unarmed defense against an armed aggressor), or in *bugei* (art of armed combat). Other distinctions also exist between each ryu, and the divisions in the branches called *ha* that created other *ryugi* (styles of practice).

Every ryu proclaimed itself to be invincible in combat, and the various clans often challenged one another in encounters called *dojo arashi* (the storm that folds

in the place of study). All *ryusha* (students) of a ryu headed to a rival ryu with their sensei and battled to test the efficiency of their style; the defeated ryu lost its honor and its students abandoned the losing school to follow the victor.

The oldest codification of a Japanese combat form is *sumo*, the traditional fight linked to the rites of Shinto (a religion without gods, which venerates the principles of the sun, earth, stones, plants, and all other aspects of nature). During the Kamakura period (1185–1333), the bushi reworked existing unarmed combat techniques (inspired by the old art of *kumi uchi*, a contact technique that requires opponents to hold onto each another) into a revised set of techniques. These revisions would adopt the title of ju jitsu.

The Use of Ju Jitsu in the Past

The bushi or, more precisely, the samurai, used ju jitsu to beat their opponents and, often, to kill them without using weapons. This method of combat complemented those that used weapons, such as *ken jutsu* (art of the saber, an important part of training for the bushi and samurai, especially in the tenth century).

Despite having a basic foundational technique, the *kyuba no michi* (art of the bow and horsemanship), the ryusha of different ryu trained in specific specialities of combat depending on the skill and knowledge of their soke.

Here are some examples of the different ryu:

Aio ryu: A ju jitsu style founded in the seventeenth century, specializing in the *yari* (lance).

Araki ryu: A style founded in the seventeenth century, specializing in *kusari gama* (sickle with chain) and ken jutsu. The ryusha used the *shinai* (bamboo sabers) for training, then the *shirobo* (wooden sabers covered in white cloth) in ken jutsu as well as *kendo* (way of the saber).

Hokushin itto ryu: A style founded in the eighteenth century, specializing in ken jutsu but with a more spiritual attitude than other ryu. Ryusha trained with *bokken* (wooden sabers) and arm protection.

Jikishin ryu: A style founded by Terada Kanemon in the eighteenth century, specializing in the study of ju jitsu. It was the first ryu to introduce non-fatal techniques to judo.

Katori shinto ryu: A style founded in the fourteenth century, specializing in ken jutsu and *bojutsu* (the art of handling a long baton), using the *naginata* (a Japanese halberd of two or three meters). It was strongly linked to the Zen religion (a Japanese school of philosophy).

Kito ryu: A style founded in the seventeenth century, specializing in ken jutsu, bojutsu, *iaijutsu* (the art of drawing the sword and striking), and ju jitsu.

Muso jiken ryu: A style founded in the sixteenth century, specializing in iaijutsu.

Tenjin shinyo ryu: A branch (ha) of the *yoshin ryu,* founded around the sixteenth century. This ryu specialized in *atemi* (strikes with upper and lower extremities), *osae* (immobilization of the opponent's body), and *shime* (chokes) techniques.

Yoshin ryu: A style founded by Akyama Shinobu, a doctor from Nagasaki who learned *kappo* techniques (the art of resuscitating an unconscious person) in China. Shinobu was inspired by the willow bending under the weight of snow, and when he returned to Japan, he dedicated himself to ju jitsu techniques based in *nage waza* (protection techniques) rather than moves that directly confronted an opponent's force.

Depending on the specific needs of each ryu and its ryusha, different knowledge and techniques were taught. Here are some examples of the various skills and specializations of different ryu:

Ho jutsu (firearms): A form that is part of the *kobudo* (ancient martial arts with unconventional weapons).

Hojo jutsu (the art of tying): Teaches to quickly immobilize an opponent by tying them up.

This is a technique used in the times of the ninja (the invisible warriors of the darkness) and is taught today to some specialized police departments in Japan.

Juken jutsu (the art of using a rifle with a bayonet): First practiced in the seventeenth century, with a major period of activity during the early years of the First World War, when Japan fought as an ally with Italy, France, and England.

Kyusho (vital points): The bushi should be familiar with all the vulnerable points on the human body to know how to definitively neutralize an opponent.

Tameshi giri (the art of cutting): This training is based in cutting rolls of rice or green bamboo canes with swords to check the true effectiveness of a given technique of ken jitsu. In the Edo period, however, it was recommended that samurais test the strength of their katana on a human body, carrying out death sentences or asserting the *kirisute gomen* (right to kill with impunity).

The Spread of Ju Jitsu

The spread of the ryu of ju jitsu throughout Japan was fundamentally linked with the *ronin* (leaderless samurais), who permanently served neither a *shogun* (a general, supreme governor directly appointed by the emperor) nor a *daimyo*

(Great Name, leader of a clan or governor of a province). The ronin created a ryu and spread the knowledge of the martial arts and their experience in real combat acquired on battlefields.

Therefore, ju jitsu was, in its founding principles, an art or technique employed to neutralize and eliminate one or more opponents. Sadly, it was also converted into a powerful offensive instrument in the hands of those who used it inappropriately, like bandits and assassins employed by the *jonin* (crime lords). Consequently, ju jitsu was widely and for many years considered an instrument of aggression.

With the improvement and spread of firearms at the end of the nineteenth century, the study of ju jitsu lost its importance, and the ryusha disappeared.

Many senseis died without the opportunity to bequeath the densho or their own knowledge to a disciple; others joined new disciplines with other sokes, such as Jigoro Kano, Gichin Funakoshi, and Morihei Ueshiba. Ju jitsu was disappearing.

Luckily, many ju jitsu ryu survived this dark period and, with a reinvigorated spirit for the study of the tradition, focused on the philosophical concept of universal prosperity and peace while simultaneously combating the concept of violence and death. Ju jitsu was revived and was once again appreciated as a life philosophy as well as a martial discipline, recuperating the moral value and ethics that had been lost for a long time.

The New Era of Ju Jitsu

In the era before the restoration of the Meiji period (1868), close to one thousand different ryu were counted, some with thousands of ryusha and others with just a few dozen. In 1843, the shogun organized and gave the schools an official character by ordering that the *bujutsu ryu soroku* (treaty of the schools of the art of combat) be written so that the 159 most important ryu could be identified.

Even today the Japanese authorities elect forty-six ryu every year to represent the different ryugi in the *taikai* (an exhibition of traditional martial arts) that celebrates in the *budokan* (the place students study and practice martial arts) of Tokyo. Ju jitsu ryu are in continuous technical evolution. The study to perfect a style does not come just from a desire to improve, but also from necessity, as in the past, for those who use this art for specific purposes, like the police or other specialized groups. In recent years, ju jitsu has been effectively affirmed as a valid technical support for those who study self-defense.

Despite this, it is interesting to note that, in 1947, the experts of the Japanese police created the *taiho jutsu* (method of attack and defense), which combined ju jitsu techniques with other diverse martial disciplines to aid public policy interventions and protect the public against criminals. Taiho jutsu includes many techniques of the *taihen jutsu* (art of moving silently), *keibo soho* (techniques for using the short baton, created for defense), *tokushu keibo* (extending baton), and others that appear and are constantly refined.

Defense Techniques and Legal Responsibility

T he significant increase of ju jitsu students is clearly linked to the high demand for self-defense courses we see today. And what other technique can better satisfy this need!

The efficiency of the ju jitsu program is interesting and surprising. It encompasses all types of technical movements, including throws, strikes, and joint levers, all applied in hand-to-hand combat at short distances.

Ju jitsu techniques that are correctly taught constitute a system of valid and efficient self-defense because of their technical characteristics and response to aggression.

Ju jitsu teachers must transmit the fundamental points of this martial art to their students, putting special emphasis on the ethical and educational aspects of the tradition of the ancient ryu and on a spirit of collaboration that allows students to learn and progress together.

With this in mind, students of ju jitsu should understand that the techniques they learn during the course of their studies have the ability to cause injury or harm to another person if employed carelessly or with malicious intent. Instructors should always model responsible behavior and urge students to use their skills conscientiously. Part of learning ju jitsu as self-defense requires practitioners to learn about the risks and laws regarding physical force.

Criminal Liability During Training

Students should be aware that participation in a combat or self-defense sport requires a level of consent to risk or injury during training. While skilled instructors will always seek to provide their students with a safe learning environment to minimize these risks, an injury-free space is never guaranteed.

However, in the event that an injury occurs and does not seem to fit within the risk a student knows he or she will face in class, criminal liability may be assessed. For example, if an instructor uses excessive force on a student with the intent to inflict harm, this no longer falls within the bounds of consented risk and therefore may be considered criminal.

The Right to Defend Yourself

Our judicial system recognizes the use of personal defense techniques within certain limits.

The criminal code in many countries requires that the citizen who commits an act usually considered unlawful (and, therefore, criminal or an offense) such as striking, causing injury, and killing, should not be punished for the action when it is committed in legitimate self-defense.

The circumstances that justify the use of defensive techniques (normally prohibited due to their wrongful potential) often legally fall into the category of exonerating circumstance. In cases such as these, a person may defend himself, provided that he was faced with a legitimate act of aggression, and the defensive actions used to impede the aggressions were necessary and rational.

Furthermore, the person claiming self-defense must also prove that the aggressor had intent to cause harm or injury and that the aggression was legally unjustifiable (namely, that it would have resulted in the endangerment of the defender's life).

Self-defense should in no way be a reaction to a justified past action (for example, if the aggressor has already gone away); this is considered revenge or retaliation.

In the same way, neither should it be a pre-emptive strike against a possible future danger, because in such a case the state or authorities can often be called in to mediate.

A person cannot invoke self-defense as a legal protection

if he instigated a fight with a person or challenged a person with the intent to offend or cause bodily harm.

Finally, self-defense should always be proportional to the act of aggression and a last resort. The defender must prove that there was no other way of avoiding the situation and that the actions taken against the aggressor were not extreme or inappropriate given the circumstances of the situation.

In the case of using self-defense techniques that surpass these limits we have just mentioned, the person who acts defensively must be held responsible as guilty of a crime, but with the concurrence of extenuating circumstances.

First Aid
During Training

During ju jitsu practice many different accidents can happen. Most of the time they are just mild situations, but some cases can be very serious and require medical assistance after the necessary first aid is administered.

Being able to recognize the difference between a simple contusion and a more serious injury can prevent an accident from becoming complicated. For this reason, we will quickly list the most frequent ju jitsu injuries.

Contusion: A contusion is a light form of trauma; it is characterized by localized swelling of the skin's epidermal layer. This swelling is followed by the appearance of bruises caused by ruptured blood cells. Bruising can be superficial or deep and is caused by trauma, normally from a blow or shock. Generally bruises will go away in a few days if you take care and immediately apply ice and a medically prescribed ointment to the area.

Training centers are required to provide packets of instant ice or cryogenic aerosols for these situations.

Obviously, when the contusion occurs in a delicate area of the body (head, eyes, ears, genitals, etc.), it will need to be handled medically, and it is always advisable to seek a doctor when the severity of an injury is in question.

Sprain: An injury to the ligaments of a joint (such as the ankle, wrist, knee, or elbow) caused by extreme twisting or wrenching.

When you get a sprain, pain and swelling are inevitable.

Aside from treating the injury with ice and anti-inflammatory medicine, it's best to immobilize the joint immediately, even if you have to use improvised materials (belts, scarves, rigid cardboard, etc.) before reaching a medical professional.

Dislocation: A dislocation occurs when there is extreme displacement of the joints. The most commonly affected areas in martial arts are the shoulder and the elbow, which, in the simplest cases, are treated by resetting the joints. Besides swelling and intense pain, dislocation is characterized by the complete impossibility of moving the injured joint.

In these cases, injuries produced in the tissues and surrounding joints are grave, and a medical professional must be consulted to reset them. But while waiting to see a doctor, it's necessary to very cautiously immobilize the joint as you would a sprain.

Fracture: This is a crack or break of a bone segment caused by direct or indirect trauma strong enough to overcome the bone's natural resistance. Fractures can be simple (closed) when the break is just a partial segment of the bone, or compound (open) when the break is complete.

Simple fractures occur when parts of the bone stay aligned and in contact, and compound fractures happen when the bone segments lose contact and push against each other. In this case the fracture is complete, and the compound fracture can be seen at the site of the laceration where part of the bone emerges from the skin.

In order to distinguish between a fracture and another kind of trauma, you must pay attention to the affected area (swelling, altered mobility, deformities) and to the indications that it will show (pain, lack of functionality).

In the case of fractures, the procedure for treatment can range from immobilization of the broken bone to surgery. In any case, first aid before medical assistance always consists of immobilization and the application of ice to the area.

Wounds: This is a traumatic injury characterized by a continuous abrasion of the skin (superficial wound) and, in more severe cases, of interior tissues (deep wound). A wound needs to be carefully cleaned and disinfected at the site. If there is a lot of blood, contact emergency medical services immediately.

Ju Jitsu Class

Like other Japanese martial arts, ju jitsu is practiced in a dojo (literally, "the place where the way and the method is studied"). Students train on a series of joined *tatami* (thin mattresses, formerly made from rice straw), which are necessary to soften any falls.

Teachers and students wear the *keikogi*, or *jutsugi*, which consist of a kimono and pants, generally white and made from a resistant material. The suit of the *jujitsuka* (practicioner of ju jitsu) is complete with a belt (called an *obi*), which will be a certain color depending on the student's experience and skill. While studying the ancient *kata* (the forms), the student will learn self-defense techniques that include personal protection and weapons at certain stages of training.

Ju jitsu students are divided according to their degree of preparation. The *kyu*, which represent the level of ability the student has achieved, goes from sixth degree to first degree and corresponds to the different belt colors:

6. white belt

5. yellow belt

4. orange belt

3. green belt

2. blue belt

1. brown belt

On the other hand, the ten levels of *dan* are the levels of the black belt in the order of ascension.

It is convenient to remember that the amount of time a student stays at each level varies according to the school. In our opinion, it

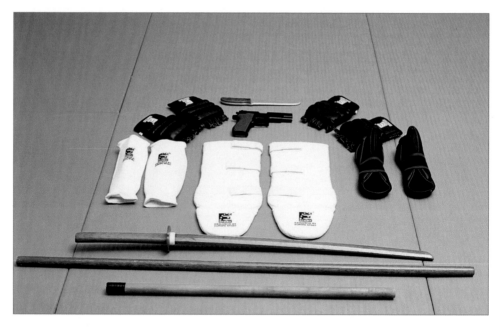

The protective gear and weapons used during training.

should not be less than one year for the lower levels, until the second degree kyu, and no less than two years in the first degree kyu.

As for the black belt, the rule says that to pass each grade, it is necessary to acquire experience equal to the number of the dan plus one (for example, three years for the second degree dan; four years for the third degree dan, etc.).

Between twelve and fourteen years is considered the ideal age to begin practicing ju jitsu, although this should be regarded flexibly. Of course, nothing impedes someone who wants to begin ju jitsu at a more mature age. Furthermore, in this sense, the experience for adult students is often very positive.

There is also nothing wrong with beginning the practice at a younger age, on the condition that the study of the techniques is proposed as a game and combined with a preliminary activity, especially so it doesn't ignore the general physical preparation phase, which is the primary objective for young athletes.

Adequate warm-up exercises prevent the risk of injury during long stretches of physical activity.

As in any activity, a thorough knowledge of ju jitsu is not possible without consistent training. Two to three sessions a week of an hour or an hour and a half are enough.

A normal class begins with the *zarei*, the traditional knee salute done between the student and the teacher. The zarei is followed by a warm-up phase, general at first and specific later, with movements essential for practice and discipline.

This warm-up phase shouldn't be underestimated, because with it, one achieves the physical conditioning necessary to address the more technical and labor-intensive tasks that follow, safe from accidents and early exhaustion.

After warming up, students practice basic techniques in pairs (striking techniques, throws, joint levers, chokes, etc.), followed by a more complete phase, like the study of the kata or self-defense sequences until the class finally culminates with real combat.

Combat is the final phase of training in a gym.

The time dedicated to each phase depends on different factors: the necessity of students to train for competition, the preparation of exams in order to move up to the next level or for exhibitions, the age of the students and their level of preparation, etc. The class ends with a stretching phase and the final salute.

Structure of a Normal Class

- *Zarei*: Traditional greeting on the knees at the beginning of the class between the students and the teacher.

- *Taiso:* Warm-up exercises for the muscles and joint mobility.

- Study of the *ukemi waza:* the technique of breaking a fall.

- *Butsukari:* Training and practice of the techniques performed in motion.

- Study of the fundamental techniques: *atemi waza* (striking techniques), *nage waza* (throwing techniques), *osae waza* (control techniques), *kansetsu waza* (dislocation techniques), and *shime waza* (choking techniques).

- Study of the techniques of the Bianchi method.

- Study of the *kata* (technical forms and sequences).

- Study of the self-defense techniques.

- *Kumite:* Combat with the use of the *atemi waza*.

- *Randori:* Combat with the use of the *nage waza*.

- *Ne waza:* Combat with the use of the *osae, kansetsu* and *shime waza*.

- *Taiso*: Muscle stretching.

- *Zarei*: Traditional salute on the knees at the end of the class between the students and the teacher.

Basic Fundamental Techniques

T he fundamental movements that appear in this chapter are important to master because they constitute the basis of the complex technical sequences we will review later.

Kamae: Guards

The guard positions vary according to the style of ju jitsu practiced, and every school has its own technical characteristics, which the teacher conveys to the students. This being said, we can note the three fundamental principles between all the possible postures:

- Adopt a natural attitude with your body balanced and stable on your legs, avoiding any tension on the extremities; the body must be ready to perform quick movements, stops, grasps, and counterattacks.
- Correctly protect the body with your arms, which shouldn't be too high in the guard position so as to limit visibility.
- Look at your opponent, taking full advantage of your lateral vision, which allows for the guard. Do not fixate on a precise point on your opponent, because the attack can be performed with any part of the body, so concentrate quickly on the surrounding environment.

It is pivotal to correctly position the body in order to appropriately respond to any attack. With practice, every person finds the position best suited to his physical characteristics and technical knowledge. The guard can also vary depending on the modality of the attack and the opponent's characteristics. We see a few examples of this in the following images.

GUARD WITH FISTS CLOSED

CLASSIC GUARD IN WAIT (of Kata)

OPEN-HANDED GUARD WITH EIGHTY PERCENT OF THE WEIGHT ON THE BACK LEG

KNEE GUARD WITH OPEN HAND

The Kata

The kata (the forms or technical sequences) exist in every martial art and are imaginary combats formed by basic movements and techniques executed in slow, correct form. They are studied to better understand the essence of a specific martial style, to obtain a technical improvement, and for purely aesthetic reasons (in fact, the theory of the kata argues for the beauty of the technical gesture). The kata are defined as the martial choreography of attacks and defenses and constitute the formal ritual of the technical performance of movements. The *waza* (techniques), on the other hand, represent the practical applications of the moves. There also exists a spiritual and philosophical aspect in the interpretation of the martial techniques defined as *do*.

All of the kata should begin and end with a greeting to the *kamiza* (seat of the *kami*), to the teachers, fellow students, and the public.

Ukemi Waza: Falling Techniques

The teaching of the falling techniques is common in all combat disciplines, with the goal of controlling the body during the takedown. This is an essential element of the study of ju jitsu to avoid injuries during practice.

In these falling techniques, it is fundamental to control the head and avoid hitting it hard against the floor, suffering traumas that hinder the ability to react.

During the education of controlled falls, it's necessary to bring the chin close to the chest and look down at the abdomen, allowing the arm or both arms to hit the floor first. If performed correctly, the impact of the fall will be absorbed by the body.

Learning the falling techniques is also important for the goal of self-defense: the student has confidence in unusual and risky situations (like those in which the attacked person falls to the floor) and is able to quickly recover back to the standing guard position (which gives the student time to react before another attack).

USHIRO UKEMI (Backward Fall)

This controlled fall avoids trauma to the shoulders, spine, legs, and, most importantly, head.

YOKO UKEMI (Side Fall)

This controlled fall helps to avoid trauma to the shoulders, pelvis, parts of the spine, legs, and head.

ZEMPO KAITEN UKEMI (Fall with Somersault Forward over the Shoulder)

In this somersault fall forward, it's important that the front arm and shoulder form a curved line to prevent any trauma to the performer. This controlled fall helps avoid trauma to the shoulder, back, legs, and face.

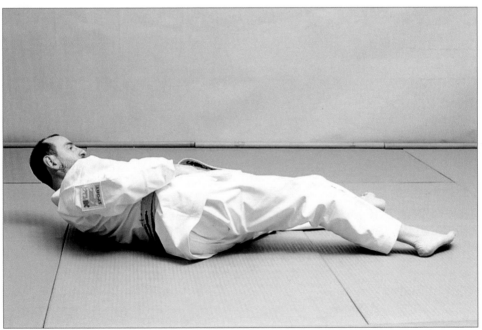

SOMERSAULT BACKWARD ENDING ON THE KNEES

To perform this somersault, it's necessary to move the head to one side and bring the legs to the opposite side. This controlled movement helps avoid trauma to the shoulders, back, legs, and head.

SOMERSAULT BACKWARD ENDING ON ONE KNEE WITH THE OTHER LEG EXTENDED

The head must be moved to one side and the legs brought to the opposite side. This controlled movement helps avoid trauma to the shoulders, back, legs, and head.

SOMERSAULT BACKWARD ENDING FACE DOWN

The head must be moved to one side and the legs brought to the opposite side. This controlled movement helps avoid trauma to the shoulders, back, legs, and head.

SOMERSAULT BACK ENDING ON THE FEET

Using the momentum of the fall, push the feet upward and back in order to roll over the head and stand back up. This controlled movement helps avoid trauma to the shoulders, back, legs, and head.

MAE UKEMI (Forward Fall)

The arms must be moved in front of the body with the palms facing forward. This controlled movement helps avoid trauma to the face, abdomen, and arms.

IMPULSIVE FORWARD FALL

Place the hands in front of the body in order to absorb the impact of the fall. Use the hands as a spring to help push the torso back up. This controlled fall helps avoid trauma to the shoulders, back, legs, and head.

Atemi Waza: Striking Techniques

The use of atemi in ju jitsu techniques and in self-defense provides a perfect control of the applied force, so that the same strike can be performed in various manners.

In this way we can perform a strike as an obstacle, to debilitate, or to conclude the technique. The first two—strike as an obstacle and to debilitate—are recommended in the practice of the traditional techniques of ju jitsu (which, let's not forget, are imbued with the principle of malleability) and in more specific applications of self-defense. In ju jitsu there is a great variety of strikes that can be performed with both the upper and lower extremities. Let's take a look at the most well-known:

OI TSUKI (Direct Strike with the Fist with Leg of the Same Side Forward)

GYAKU TSUKI (Direct Strike with the Fist Opposite the Forward Leg)

MAWASHI TSUKI (Circular Fist Strike with the Leg in an Open Position)

URAKEN (Strike with the Back of the Fist)

EMPI (Forward and Upward Elbow Strike)

DOWNWARD ELBOW STRIKE

SIDE ELBOW STRIKE

CIRCULAR ELBOW STRIKE

BACKWARD ELBOW STRIKE

SHUTO (Inward Open-Hand Circular Strike)

OUTWARD OPEN-HAND CIRCULAR STRIKE

HAITO (Inward Open-Hand Circular Strike with the Inside of the Hand)

OUTWARD OPEN-HAND CIRCULAR STRIKE WITH INSIDE

TEISHO (Strike with the Palm of the Hand)

MAE GERI (Front Kick)

MAWASHI GERI (Circular Kick)

YOKO GERI (Side Kick)

URA MAWASHI GERI (Inverse Circular Kick)

USHIRO GERI (Backward Kick)

KAKATO GERI (Downward Kick with the Heel)

HIZA GERI (Upward Knee Strike)

SIDEWAYS KNEE STRIKE

Uke Waza: Blocking and Evasion Techniques

In ju jitsu, the block is normally used to evade or avoid direct impact; it allows students to perform a given technique in its entirety. Some of these blocks can be used against different attacks like punches, or kicks.

For a correct execution of the blocks, the distance between the person performing the technique and the aggressor is of special interest; of course, the dynamic with which the blow is deflected is also essential.

Here we've listed some of the most common blocks.

HIGH BLOCK WITH SAME LEG FORWARD

HIGH BLOCK WITH OPPOSITE LEG FORWARD

HIGH BLOCK CROSSING THE ARMS

LOW BLOCK CROSSED

MIDDLE BLOCK FROM THE INSIDE OUTWARD

Kansetsu Waza: Levers and Joint Torsions

In all the styles and schools of ju jitsu, students study levers and twists in order to understand how to control the body. This knowledge is fundamental in taking down an opponent.

Levers and twists should only be used in extreme cases, as they have the possibility of dislocating an extremity if they are performed with too much force.

For this reason, we only show the most common techniques here, especially those focused on the upper limbs.

KOTE GAESHI (Twisting the Wrist Outward)

IKKYO (Twisting the Wrist Inward with Arm Extended)

KOTE MAWASHI (Twisting the Wrist Inward, Bending the Arm, and Pushing It Down)

SHIHO NAGE (Twisting the Wrist and Passing Below the Arm)

WAKI GATAME (Elbow Lever with Lock Under Armpit)

UDE GARAMI (Shoulder Lever Rotating the Arm)

WRIST LEVER WITH THE ARM STRETCHED

Nage Waza: Throwing Techniques

To correctly perform throws, one must understand the fundamental importance of unbalancing the opponent.

You can unbalance an opponent through the direct action of pushing or traction, or by taking advantage of the moment of instability that the aggressor finds himself in during the attack.

In the field of personal defense, the unbalance is often carried out by the use of a lever, choke, and atemi.

The throws that we are going to illustrate are fundamental for almost all technical sequences. They should be intensely studied and practiced in order to perform them correctly and securely during a counterattack. The throw is also the most visually spectacular moment of the diverse sequences of defense used in ju jitsu.

O SOTO GARI (Tackle with Outer Lever)

O UCHI GARI (Tackle with Inner Lever)

KO SOTO GARI KO SOTO GARI (Little Tackle with the Outer Lever)

DE ASHI BARAI
(Forward Leg Sweep)

SASAE TSURI KOMI ASHI (Turning and Lifting Ankle Block)

O GOSHI (Big Key)

KOSHI GURUMA (Rotation over the Hip)

HARAI GOSHI (Hip Sweep)

IPPON SEOI NAGE (Shoulder Throw)

TAI OTOSHI (Arm Throw with Body Fall)

Shime Waza: Choking Techniques

Mastering the choking techniques is of paramount importance in the application of ju jitsu if the goal is self-defense. The choking actions can be divided into two groups: those performed with bare hands, and those performed with the help of objects (items that may be readily available at the moment of an attack, such as a belt or tie).

We are going to show four types of choking techniques that, while shown here from a standing position, can also be performed when fighting on the ground.

HADAKA JIME (Choking with Bare Hands)

NAMI JUJI JIME (Choking with Hands Crossed and the Thumbs Inward)

GYAKU JUJI JIME (Choking with Hands Crossed and Thumbs on the Outside)

KATA JUJI JIME (Choking with Hands Crossed, One Thumb on the Outside and the Other Facing Inward)

Bare-Handed Defense Techniques Against an Unarmed Aggressor

The moment to try the technical sequences has arrived. We will join the fundamental techniques together to form an effective defense against different possible attacks.

All of the studied sequences begin with students in the guard position, so this image will not be shown every time. The technical sequences can be divided into two types: bare-handed defense against unarmed attacks and bare-handed defense with the use of everyday objects.

We want to insist again that the only way to achieve an effective physical, mental, and technical preparation is to repeat the technical gestures and movements necessary for a correct performance.

Do not get tired of practicing the same movement; try to perfect it until you can do it with your eyes closed.

The guard position serves as the starting position for all technical sequences.

Remember that it is one thing to try the technical movements with a partner with whom you have confidence and do not fear, and it is another thing to be subjected to the stress of being attacked by one or multiple unknown opponents

and to confront a very dangerous situation.

Practicing daily in a gym also helps develop the necessary characteristics of self-control and the correct physical response to external actions. So, get to work!

FIRST DEFENSE AGAINST A DIRECT PUNCH TO THE FACE

1. Rotate on the point of the right foot, moving clockwise with the left leg and getting out of the trajectory and scope of the opponent's attack.

2. Rotate the hips clockwise. Grip your opponent's right wrist with your right hand and, at the same time, grab the opponent's neck with your left arm.

3. Stretch the arm of your opponent in front of your chest and use your left arm to choke, pulling the top part of the lapel.

4. Perform a large counterclockwise rotation, using the right foot like a point of support; support your left knee on the ground. Follow with the choke and create a lever with your opponent's right elbow.

SECOND DEFENSE AGAINST A DIRECT PUNCH TO THE FACE

1. Move forward with the right leg toward the interior of your opponent's attack and grasp his right wrist with your left hand.

2. Destabilize your opponent by moving forward and turn his neck with your right arm.

3. Rotate your opponent's entire body and set your weight on his right hip; strike the right leg, moving it away from you.

4. After throwing the opponent to the ground, hold onto his arm, stretching it and dislocating it with your right knee; punch the opponent in the face with your right fist.

THIRD DEFENSE AGAINST A DIRECT PUNCH TO THE FACE

1. Keep your left leg back and divert the attack by grabbing the opponent's right wrist with your right hand.

2. Place your left leg behind the opponent's right leg. Hold his punching arm with your right hand and twist it, pushing forward.

3. At the same time, perform a large turn clockwise and, with the left foot as the point of support, take your opponent down.

4. After throwing him face down, block his right shoulder with your left knee and control the right arm with a joint lever.

EXTERIOR DEFENSE AGAINST AN OPEN-HANDED CIRCULAR STRIKE TO THE NECK

1. Move your right leg forward to the opponent's area of attack and block with your left forearm.

2. While pulling the opponent's arm down and inward, strike the opponent's neck with the edge of your hand.

3. Now move your left leg forward to the right and, with your back to your opponent, twist his arm, making a lever with his right shoulder.

4. Incline your body, make a 180º turn, and bring the opponent's elbow to the side of his head. Using your right arm like a baton, take him down.

5. Move the left leg forward and, pressing the opponent's right armpit with your right knee, control his elbow with your left hand and prepare to punch his face with your right arm.

INTERIOR DEFENSE AGAINST AN OPEN-HANDED CIRCULAR STRIKE TO THE NECK

1. Turn your left leg outward and divert the attack inward.

2. Grab the opponent's right wrist and twist it upward; immediately after, move your left leg forward, pushing the opponent down while moving his elbow forward.

3. Always keep hold of the wrist above the shoulder. Move the left leg forward and stretch the opponent's right arm.

4. With this gentle move, you can push your opponent facedown to the ground; keep control of the right shoulder with your left knee, increasing the twist on the wrist.

FIRST DEFENSE AGAINST A DIRECT PUNCH TO THE ABDOMEN

1. Move your right leg forward. Place it inside the attack position of the opponent and stop the punch with your left forearm.

2. Rotate the attacker's arm with your left arm and, placing the forearm on his neck, hold his shoulder with your right hand. Take him down by making a lever with his right arm.

3. Finally, move the left leg forward, bringing the knee against the inside part of the opponent's right leg and punch him in the abdomen.

SECOND DEFENSE AGAINST A DIRECT PUNCH TO THE ABDOMEN

1. Stop the opponent's fist with your right forearm.

2. Move your left leg inward into the area of attack, turning 180° clockwise and using your right foot as a point of support. Grab the opponent's wrist with both hands and place your left arm below the attacker's elbow to make a lever, forcing him to lift over the point of the feet.

3. Pass under the opponent's arm, casting the right arm backward; increase the twist and the traction on the attacker's wrist, forcing him to fall forward.

4. Support your right knee on the ground and control your opponent, making a lever with his arm.

FIRST DEFENSE AGAINST A FRONT KICK TO THE ABDOMEN

1. Move the right leg forward and into the attack; stop it with your left forearm, hooking the opponent's right leg from below.

2. At the same time, grab his right shoulder with your right hand and throw him by sweeping with an inside lever against the left leg.

3. Push your opponent to the ground without dropping his right leg.

4. Stretch the leg upward until the opponent is forced facedown onto his left side.

5. Keep him blocked on the ground, supporting your right knee on the opponent's lumbar area and striking the shoulder with your right fist.

SECOND DEFENSE AGAINST A FRONT KICK TO THE ABDOMEN

1. Move your right leg forward into the outer area of the attack and rotate with your hip to the right, to perform a low right block with your right forearm. Grab the attacker's right arm simultaneously with your left hand.

2. Grab the opponent's lower right leg and move closer to him.

3. Throw your opponent, with your left leg supporting his weight.

4. Release the leg and completely block the right arm, pressing on the opponent's neck with your left knee.

DEFENSE AGAINST A ROUNDHOUSE KICK

1. Move your right leg forward and rotate counterclockwise with your hips to block the opponent's attack. With your right forearm, block his leg at thigh height while hooking the leg with your left arm and tightening it against your chest.

2. Without moving your right leg, move forward with the left, placing it in line with the opponent's left leg. Simultaneously make a lever from the right leg and force it to rotate.

3. Pulling him toward you and pushing downward, take the opponent down so he remains facing the floor.

4. Block his left leg with your knee and increase the lever and twisting of the right knee, placing all your weight forward.

DEFENSE AGAINST A SIDE KICK

1. Move toward the left side and get out of the kick's trajectory.

2. Circle your opponent's leg from below with your right arm and move the left leg forward to take him down, creating a lever out of the left leg.

3. Throw him to the ground, but without letting go of the leg.

4. Control the two legs and strike at the mid back.

DEFENSE AGAINST A FRONT CHOKE

1. Working from the outside, block your opponent's right hand with your left hand.

2. Move your left leg back. Perform a hook from inside outward with your right arm and strike downward at the opponent's left arm.

3. With the right leg as a point of support, continue the circular movement counterclockwise. Use the right hand as well, increase the twisting and the traction on your opponent's right wrist until he goes down.

4. Place yourself behind your opponent's head and force him to roll over, bringing your right hand up to the elbow joint and pushing down on it. Once he's facedown, bend the arm over the back.

5. To finish, block him on the floor, pressing with your left knee onto the lumbar and increasing the lever on the right elbow and shoulder.

DEFENSE AGAINST SIDE SHOULDER TAKEDOWN

1. The opponent makes a side grab on your shoulder and tries to punch you in the face with his left hand. Block the attack with your left arm.

2. Move to the right with your left leg. Surrounding the opponent's right leg with your left arm, make an upward strike to his chin with the palm of your hand.

3. To continue, take the opponent down with a lever—your right leg against his right leg.

4. When on the floor, grab your opponent and, making a lever with his arm and forcing him to rotate facedown, place yourself in front of his head pressing on his right shoulder with your right knee. Once you have it blocked, strike the opponent's neck with your right hand.

DEFENSE AGAINST A WRIST TAKEDOWN

1. The opponent grabs your left wrist, trying to strike you with his left fist.

2. Stop the punch, while making a semi-rotation upward with your left forearm to displace the pressure and grab the opponent's wrist.

3. Now move toward your opponent with the left foot: make a 180º twist, using the left foot as a point of support and lifting his right arm above your head.

4. Once your opponent has been taken down, block him by bringing your right knee to his right armpit and pressing his right elbow to the floor with your left hand; punch him in the face with your right hand.

DEFENSE AGAINST A GRAB ATTACK FROM BEHIND

1. To free yourself from the grasp, tighten your fists and bend your legs, exhaling and lifting your arms.

2. Once free, grasp the opponent's right wrist with your left hand, and grab his arm from below with your right arm.

3. Support yourself on your knee and throw your opponent.

4. Once you have him on the ground, punch his face with the back of your fist.

DEFENSE AGAINST A SIDE NECK TAKEDOWN (Lock Type)

1. The opponent tries to strangle you with his right arm; react quickly, pressing the opponent's forearm with both hands.

2. When the opponent slightly loosens the grasp on your neck, strike his lower abdomen with your right hand.

3. Rotate 180°, supporting yourself on your right foot and passing below the right arm, which is pressing on your neck. You will find yourself in front of your opponent with this move and also in control of his right arm.

4. Pressing downward and taking a step back, throw him facedown and make a lever with his right shoulder using your right knee.

Bare-Handed Defense Techniques Against an Armed Aggressor

Experiencing an attack from an armed assailant is an incredibly dangerous situation. You must always assess if your life or the lives of those around you are at risk.

Only if you are facing this situation should you think of an effective defense, and only one proportional to the actions of the perpetrator.

Therefore, try to avoid the risk of being injured in a confrontation over a few dollars or some object of value—it's not worth it. In all cases, it's important to stay calm to confront the situation in the best way possible.

FIRST DEFENSE AGAINST A STAB TO THE ABDOMEN

1. Get out of the trajectory of the knife and move to the outside. Stop the strike with your forearms crossed (the left on the inside) at the height of the opponent's wrist.

2. With both hands, grab the hand with the weapon and move forward with your left leg.

3. Now move your right leg forward and, using it as a point of support, rotate counterclockwise.

4. From this position, twist the opponent's wrist and force him down to the ground.

5. Always watch the arm holding the weapon. Bring it behind his head, forcing him to lie facedown.

6. Disarm the aggressor by bending the arm with the weapon behind his back.

SECOND DEFENSE AGAINST A STAB TO THE ABDOMEN

1. Get out of the attacker's trajectory. Move the right leg forward and toward the inside of your opponent's legs. Stop the attack with your forearms crossed (in this case, the right arm on the inside); block the aggressor's arm in a way that the knife stays away from your arm.

2. Grab the aggressor's right arm and rotate it clockwise with the left leg as a point of support.

3. Press the opponent's right shoulder down and increase the lever to push him to the ground.

4. Block and disarm your attacker.

DEFENSE AGAINST A DOWNWARD STAB

1. Move your right leg forward, anticipating the attack. Block the attack with your right arm and push backward on the arm with the weapon.

2. Force it to deviate from the direction of attack, grabbing the opponent's wrist with your right hand and his elbow with your left.

3. Move forward while putting downward pressure on the opponent's elbow and pull the wrist upward—this forces him facedown.

4. Place your left knee on his right shoulder and disarm the opponent while keeping a tight grip on the wrist.

DEFENSE AGAINST A SIDE STAB TO THE NECK

1. Move your right leg forward while moving your right arm outward, away from the attack.

2. With the right foot as a point of support, turn around to place yourself behind your opponent's back; grab his neck with your left arm.

3. Grab the wrist of the arm holding the weapon with your right hand; control your opponent by making a lever with his arm and pressing your left arm against his neck, holding the lapel.

4. Make a large rotation backward, your right foot as the point of support, and support the left knee on the ground. Continue maintaining the chokehold and increase the lever on the opponent's right elbow, forcing him to release the dagger.

DEFENSE AGAINST A DOWNWARD BATON ATTACK

1. Move forward with your right leg and left forearm to block the attack.

2. Turn around 180°, with the right foot as the point of support, turning your back to the opponent. At the same time, grab the arm holding the weapon with your left hand while surrounding the opponent's other arm with your right arm from below.

3. Throw the opponent over your shoulder, bringing him facedown on the ground.

4. Disarm the attacker by making a lever with your left knee on the arm holding the weapon.

DEFENSE AGAINST A SIDE BATON ATTACK

1. Move your right leg forward, blocking the attack with your left forearm. Strike the opponent's right bicep with your right fist.

2. Hold the opponent's right shoulder with your right hand; move your right leg until it blocks the opponent's right leg.

3. Throw your opponent to the ground and keep him facedown.

4. Disarm your attacker when he's on the ground by pushing with your right knee against the elbow of the arm holding the weapon.

FIRST DEFENSE AGAINST A GUN POINTED AT THE ABDOMEN

1. Lift your arms in a surrendering motion.

2. Turn the hips quickly clockwise and, with your left hand, grab the hand holding the gun. Push the arm downward while punching the attacker in the face to distract him.

3. Move the left leg forward while grabbing the attacker's hand holding the weapon. At no time should you ever lose sight of the gun.

4. Push the attacker to the ground, forcing him facedown. Surround the arm that holds the weapon with your left arm, locking it under your armpit. Make a lever with the joint and disarm the attacker.

SECOND DEFENSE AGAINST A GUN POINTED AT YOUR ABDOMEN

1. Move the armed hand to the left, as in the previous exercise.

2. Support yourself on your front foot, in this case the right, and turn backward 180º. Twist the wrist that holds the weapon, keeping it directed at the attacker. Take advantage of this position to take him down.

3. Place your left knee on the ground. Quickly dislocate the attacker's right wrist (the armed hand) and disarm him.

Defense Techniques with Everyday Objects

As we continue, we'll see how to react against attacks using objects we usually have with us. We should always be aware of the consequences that such an attack can cause.

DEFENSE AGAINST A DIRECT PUNCH TO THE FACE

1. Stop the attack by holding an umbrella by the handle.

2. Grab the attacker's right wrist with your left hand and push it downward while you hit him in the neck with the umbrella.

3. Rotate 180° counterclockwise with your left leg and strike your opponent's abdomen with the umbrella.

4. Place the right leg in front of your opponent to block his legs, taking him down and using the umbrella to make a lever between his neck and arm.

DEFENSE AGAINST A DISTANT ATTACK

1. Stop the opponent's attack, striking his abdomen with the umbrella.

2. Move the right leg forward while turning the umbrella; hit the attacker on the side of the neck and hook him with the handle.

3. Place your right leg in front of the opponent.

4. With the handle of the umbrella still hooked around the attacker's neck, pull the umbrella downward, and force your attacker to the ground.

DEFENSE AGAINST AN ATTEMPTED ROBBERY

1. The aggressor tries to take your bag by the strap.

2. Take a step back and turn 180º.

3. Grab the attacker's right arm with your left hand and, with the right hand holding your cell phone, hit him just under the ear.

4. Take the attacker down by making a lever with your leg and throwing him to the ground.

5. Watch for a possible reaction and block him on the ground.

DEFENSE AGAINST AN ATTEMPTED ROBBERY WITH A MELEE WEAPON

1. In this situation the attacker tries to take your handbag and threatens you with a knife.

2. Use the open umbrella as a shield and push the attacker's weapon and arm backward.

3. Kick him below the stomach with your left foot.

4. This forces him to drop the bag and fall backward.

DEFENSE AGAINST A THREAT WITH A MELEE WEAPON

1. Pretend to give the aggressor money; go through your bag and clutch your keys in your hand.

2. Grab the wrist of the hand that holds the weapon with your left hand and move it away from you.

3. Strike your attacker's face with the tips of the keys.

DEFENSE AGAINST A BATON COMING DOWNWARD

1. The attacker tries to hit you from the front with a baton.

2. Use your helmet like a shield and block the arm with the weapon, grabbing the attacker's wrist and moving your right leg forward.

119

3. Take a small step back with your right foot and, turning clockwise, pull downward on the attacker's arm. Hit him in the back of the neck with your helmet.

4. Turn counterclockwise and maintain control of the attacker on the ground, pinning him on his side and putting your left knee on his shoulder, so you can disarm him without danger.

DEFENSE AGAINST A THREAT WITH A GUN

1. The attacker threatens you with a gun, ordering you to give him your watch.

2. Do as he says and bring your arm holding the umbrella forward while using your other hand to pretend to take off the watch.

3. Take a step forward with your left leg and, at the same moment, move the arm with the weapon away. Grab the attacker's right elbow with your left hand.

4. Turn clockwise with your left foot as a point of support and block the attacker's arm with your left armpit.

5. Hit the attacker with the end of the umbrella.

6. Push the attacker forward until he falls facedown; press his arm down and disarm him, using your left knee as support on the ground.

Glossary

bojutsu   One of the core elements of classical Japanese martial arts training, which focuses on the use of a staff weapon in combat.

bushi   Another term for samurai, a Japanese warrior class who valued martial arts mastery, honor, loyalty, and frugality above all else.

iaijutsu   A Japanese quick-draw sword technique, which was part of the central education of the samurai before the Meji period.

ken jutsu   A general term that designates all forms of the study of Japanese swordsmanship, generally studied by the samurai before the Meiji period.

ryu   A general term for any martial arts school specializing in a specific series of combat techniques.

Further Reading

Books

Craig, Darrell Max. *Japanese Jiu-jitsu: Secret Techniques of Self-Defense*. North Clarendon, VT: Tuttle Publishing, 2015.

Kirby, George. *Jujitsu: Advanced Techniques for Redirecting an Opponent's Energy*. El Segundo, CA: Black Belt Communications, 2015.

Ribeiro, Saul and Kevin Howell. *Jiu-Jitsu University*. Las Vegas, NV: Victory Belt Publishing, 2015.

Websites

The American Federation of Jujitsu

www.amfedjujitsu.com

An organization founded in 1977 with the intent of uniting all schools and styles of ju jitsu into one federation.

Jiu Jitsu Global Federation

www.jjgf.com

A federation devoted to the expansion of ju jitsu throughout the world. This website offers ju jitsu athletes up-to-date news and events about the sport.

Jiu Jitsu Style

www.bjjstyle.com

An online ju jitsu magazine that highlights important news about the sport and includes an online store to purchase ju jitsu gear.

Index

A

aggression, 11, 13, 15

aio ryu, 9

araki ryu, 9

atemi, 9, 23, 38-49, 56

attack, 12, 24, 25, 27, 50, 56, 61, 63,
    64, 66, 68, 70, 72, 74, 75, 77, 79,
    81, 87, 91, 95, 98, 100, 102, 104,
    106, 111, 113

B / C

bare-handed, 63–94, 95–110

baton, 9, 12, 71, 104, 106, 119

belt, 7, 17, 19, 20, 61

blocks, 5, 50–51, 58, 69, 70, 79, 81, 90

bojutsu, 9

bokken, 9

budokan, 12

bugei, 8

bujutsu ryu soroku, 11

bukinobu, 8

bushi, 8, 9, 10

butsukari, 23

chokes, 9, 21, 23, 56, 61–62, 65,
    85, 103

contusion, 16

D / E

daimyo, 11

dan, 19, 20

densho, 7, 11

disarm, 97, 99, 101, 105, 107, 109,
    110, 120, 123

dislocation, 17, 23

dojo, 8, 13, 19

Edo period, 10

F / G / H

falls, 19, 23, 27–37, 60

first aid, 16–18

fracture, 17–18

Funakoshi, Gichin, 11

geri, 45, 46, 47, 48, 49

guards, 24–26, 27, 63

gun, 108–109, 110, 121–123

ho jutsu, 10

hojo jutsu, 10

I / J

iaijutsu, 9

injury, 14, 15, 16, 17, 18, 21

jikishin ryu, 9

jime, 61, 62

juken jutsu, 10

juko gashira, 7, 8

jutsugi, see *keigoki*

K

kamae, see guards

Kamakura period, 8

kamiza, 27

Kano, Jigoro, 11

kansetsu waza, see levers

kata, 19, 21, 23, 25, 27, 62

katana, 7, 10

katori shinto ryu, 9

keibo soho, 12

keikogi, 19

ken jitsu, 9–10

kicks, 45, 46, 47, 48, 50, 77, 79, 81, 83

kirisute gomen, 10

kito ryu, 9

kumi uchi, 8

kumite, 23

kusari gama, 9

kyu, 19–20

kyuba no michi, 9

kyusho, 10

L / M

legal responsibility, 13–15

levers, 13, 21, 52–55, 56, 57, 65, 69,
70, 74, 75, 76, 77, 81, 82, 83, 86,
88, 94, 99, 103, 105, 109, 112, 115

Meiji period, 7, 11

muso jiken ryu, 9

N / O

nage waza, see throws

naginata, 9

obi, see belt

P / R

punches, 50, 64, 66, 67, 68, 71, 74,
75, 87, 89, 90, 92, 108, 111

randori, 23

risk, 14, 27, 95

ronin, 10, 11

ryu, 7, 8, 9, 10, 11, 12, 13

S

samurai, 7, 8, 9, 10

self-defense, 5, 12, 13, 14, 15, 21, 23, 27, 38, 61

sensei, 7, 8, 11

shime waza, see chokes

shinai, 9

Shinobu, Akyama, 10

Shinto, 8

shirobo, 9

shodai, 7, 8

shogun, 11

shuto, 43

soke, 7, 8, 9, 11

somersault, 30, 32, 33, 34, 35

sprain, 16-17

stab, 95, 98, 100, 102

T

taihen jutsu, 12

taiho jutsu, 12

taiso, 23

tameshi giri, 10

tatami, 19

tenjin shinyo ryu, 9

throws, 13, 21, 23, 56–60

tokushu keibo, 12

torsions, 52–55

toshunobu, 8

tsuki, 38–39

U

ude garami, 55

Ueshiba, Morihei, 11

uke waza, see blocks

ukemi waza, see falls

unarmed, 7, 8, 63–94

V / W

violence, 6, 11

waki gatame, 55

warm up, 21, 23

waza, 10, 23, 27–37, 38–49, 50–51, 52–55, 56–60, 61–62

weapon, 7, 9, 10, 19, 50, 95–110, 116–123

wounds, 18

Y / Z

yoshin ryu, 9, 10

zarei, 21, 23

Zen, 9